GW01374456

The First Christmas

Hunt & Thorpe

What is the real Christmas story?

Not a mythical tale of tinsel and trappings,
nor even one that started in Bethlehem two thousand
years ago. Jennifer Larcombe Rees places the birth of Christ in
the context of God's unfolding plan for the world, beginning with
Creation, the Garden of Eden and the first sin that separated
people from God. Taking the angels' point of view she
vividly brings to life this real, moving and
supernatural story.

"Whatever is God doing now?" wondered
the smallest angel in Heaven. He had been most excited
as he watched God make the world, heaping up great
mountains, cutting deep valleys and smoothing wide sandy
beaches. Then he had laughed in delight at some of the funny
creatures God made next, waddling ducks, wobbly jellyfish,
wiggly caterpillars and big, bouncy kangaroos.

"But who is He making all this *for*?" he demanded.

"People," explained a larger angel. "They are going to be God's
special friends so He wants everything to be perfect
for them."

"But why does He need friends," asked the smallest angel in
surprise. "He's got all of us."

"Yes, but we're only His helpers. People are special because
they can choose," said the biggest angel.

The smallest angel did not know what
choosing meant, but he did not like to ask because the other
angels were all looking so worried.

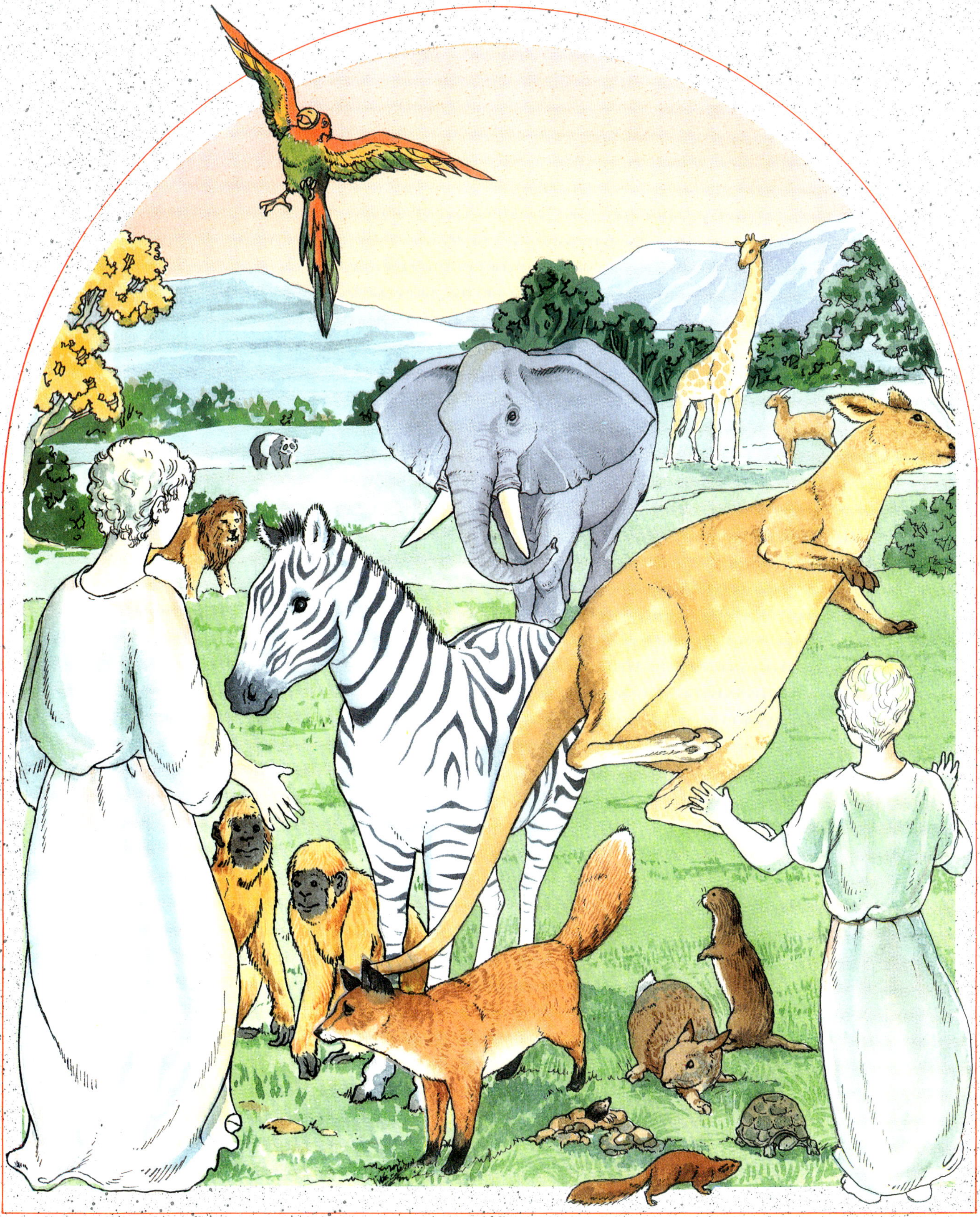

"Satan isn't going to like God making people," they whispered, and shuddered at the mention of God's great enemy. "He always tries to spoil everything."

From the dark shadows Satan also watched as God placed a man and a woman in the lovely garden He had planted for them. Satan hated to see how happy God was with His new friends Adam and Eve.

"I must put a stop to this," he said as he heard them all laughing together one evening. So next day, dressed as a snake, he slithered up to Eve as she sat alone enjoying her beautiful flowers. It was hot in the garden and she was very thirsty.

"Why not try one of those delicious juicy apples over there?" hissed Satan.

"Oh, no," replied Eve, "the only thing God says we must never do is touch those apples."

"Why should you do what God says?" grinned Satan. "Go on, have one."

All the angels in Heaven held their breath in horror. They knew what would happen if Eve listened to Satan and ate that apple.

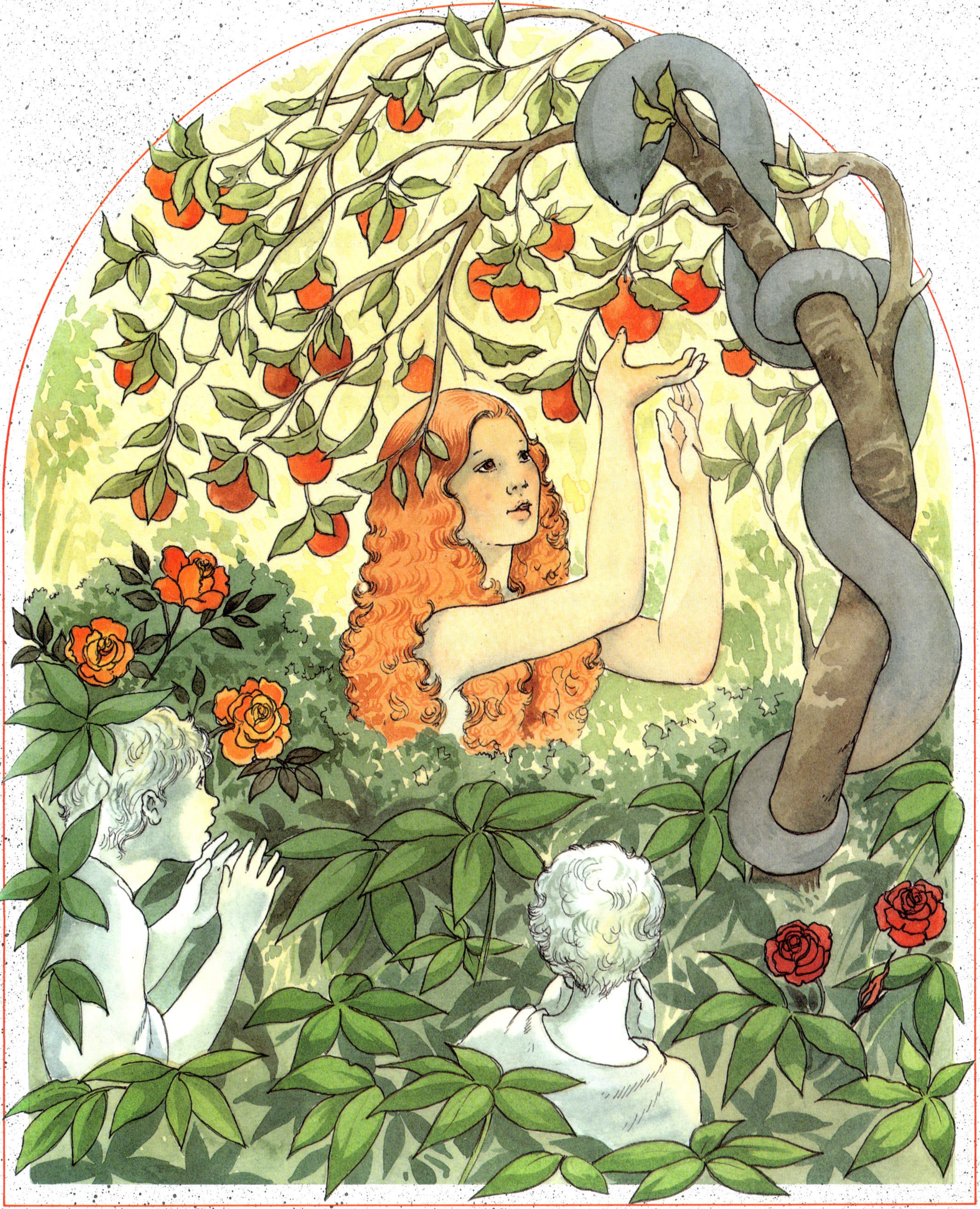

"Everything in God's lovely new world will be spoiled," sobbed the smallest angel, as Eve reached up to pick some fruit. "Why doesn't God stop her?"

"Because people can choose," replied the other angels sadly. "They can decide to be God's friends or Satan's followers."

Crunch went Eve's teeth, deep into the fruit, and soon Adam was eating an apple too.

Everything that is horrid came into the world that day. Animals became wild and fierce. Weeds and burrs and scratchy thorns began to grow everywhere. Germs developed, waiting to make people ill, and nasty thoughts and plans started to grow.

"But the worst thing of all is that now people won't be able to find their way here to Heaven," cried all the angels together.

"SATAN!" thundered God, "you think you have power now to make My people sad, but watch out! One day I will send someone into the world who will break your power and make people happy forever."

"Who will this someone be?" whispered all the angels. They had to wait a long time before they found out.

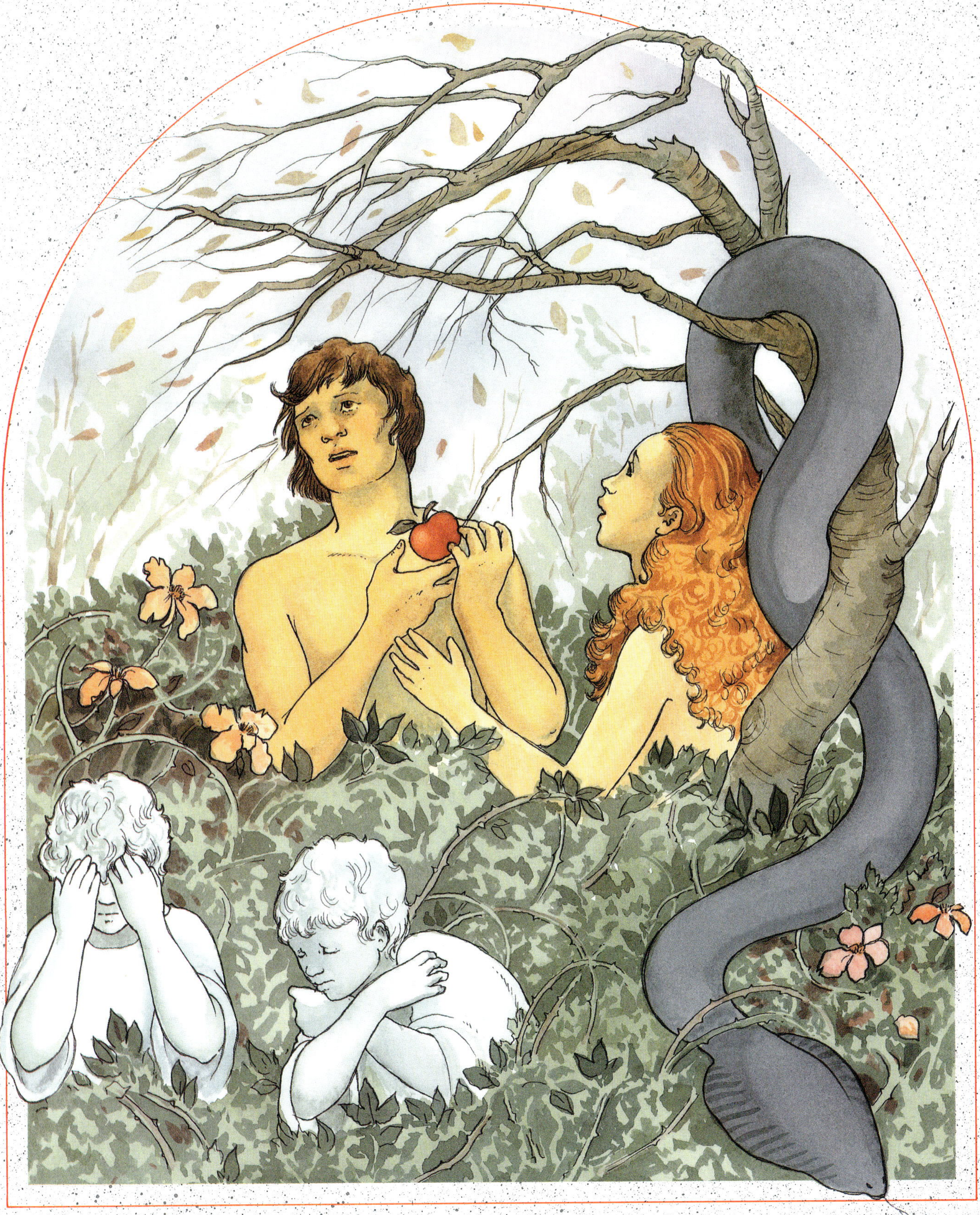

First people had to spread all over the world,
build houses, cities, ships and roads. Some of them chose to be
God's friends while others chose to follow Satan and become
horrid, mean and cruel. Over and over God sent them
messages reminding them of the Someone who was coming,
but most of them would not even listen.

"The trouble is," said the biggest angel, "people don't know
what God is really like. They think He is fierce, angry and
frightening. They don't know how gentle and kind He is."

◇

One day Heaven was full of whispers. Angels sat around
in little excited groups, and only the smallest angel was left,
hopping about, demanding to know what was happening.

"It's time for the Someone!" they told him, "and you'll
never guess who he is! God's very own Son! He's going down
to Earth to become a baby."

"God's own son, a baby!" gasped the smallest angel. "Surely
only the greatest Queen in all the world or the most beautiful
Princess would be important enough to be His mother. And
only the biggest, grandest palace will be special enough for His
birth." For once all the other angels agreed with him.

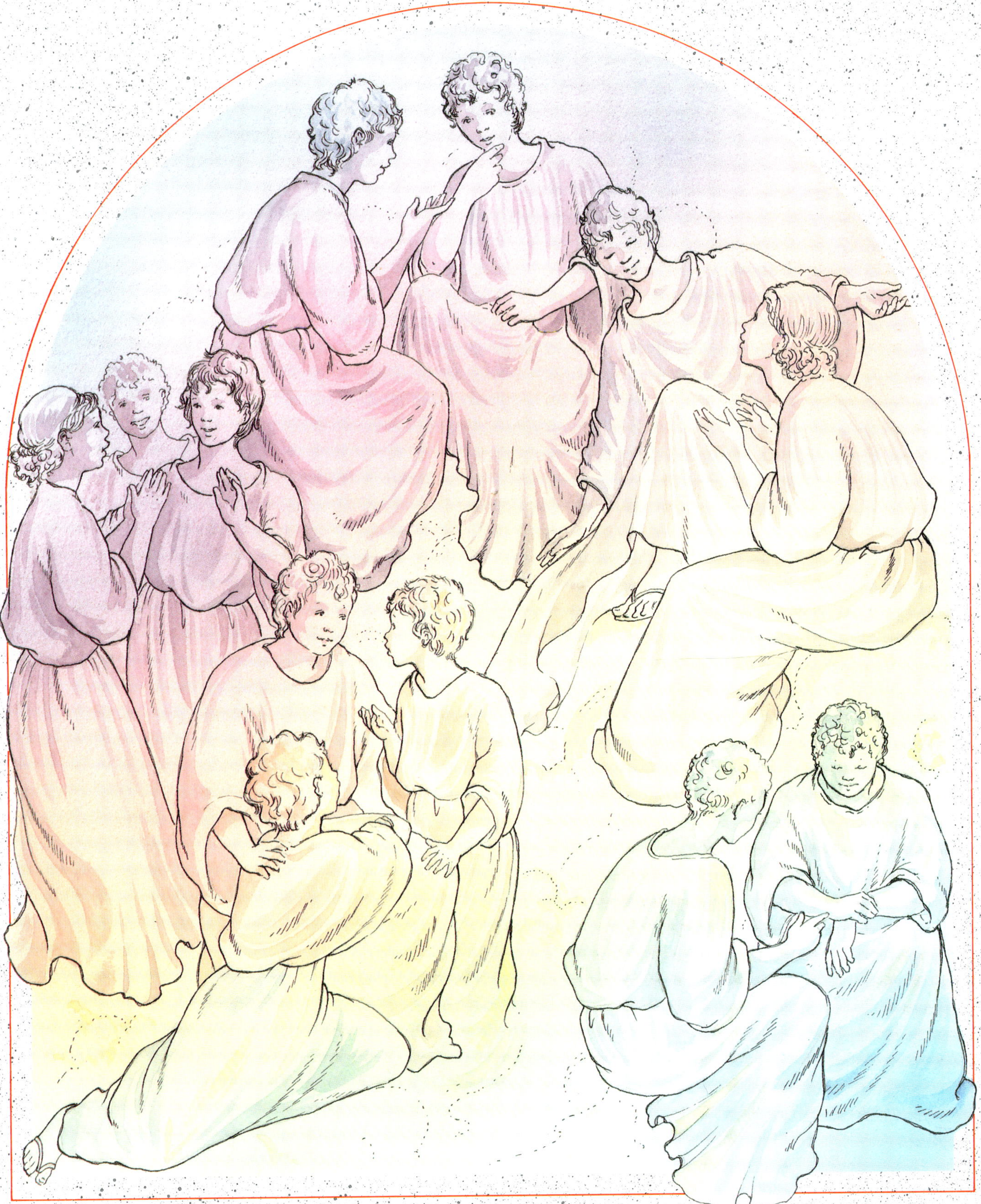

How astonished they all were when Gabriel,
the most important angel, was sent, not to a Queen or even
a Princess, but to a shabby girl who lived in a poor little house
in a forgotten village. Her name was Mary and she was sewing
her wedding dress when Gabriel appeared beside her. She was
so surprised she dropped her needle.

"You are going to be the mother of the Special Someone that
God has promised to send to this earth," said Gabriel. The
smallest angel waited to see how pleased and proud Mary
would look, but instead she only looked worried.

"How can I have God's baby?" she whispered. "I'm engaged to
be married to Joseph the village carpenter."

"Surely she wouldn't choose *not* to do this great thing for
God!" gasped all the angels in horror. But Gabriel understood
how Mary felt and gently he explained everything to her.

"Whatever God wants me to do, I will do," she said at last as
she smiled up at Gabriel.

"She's made her choice," said the angels and a sigh of relief
rippled around heaven.

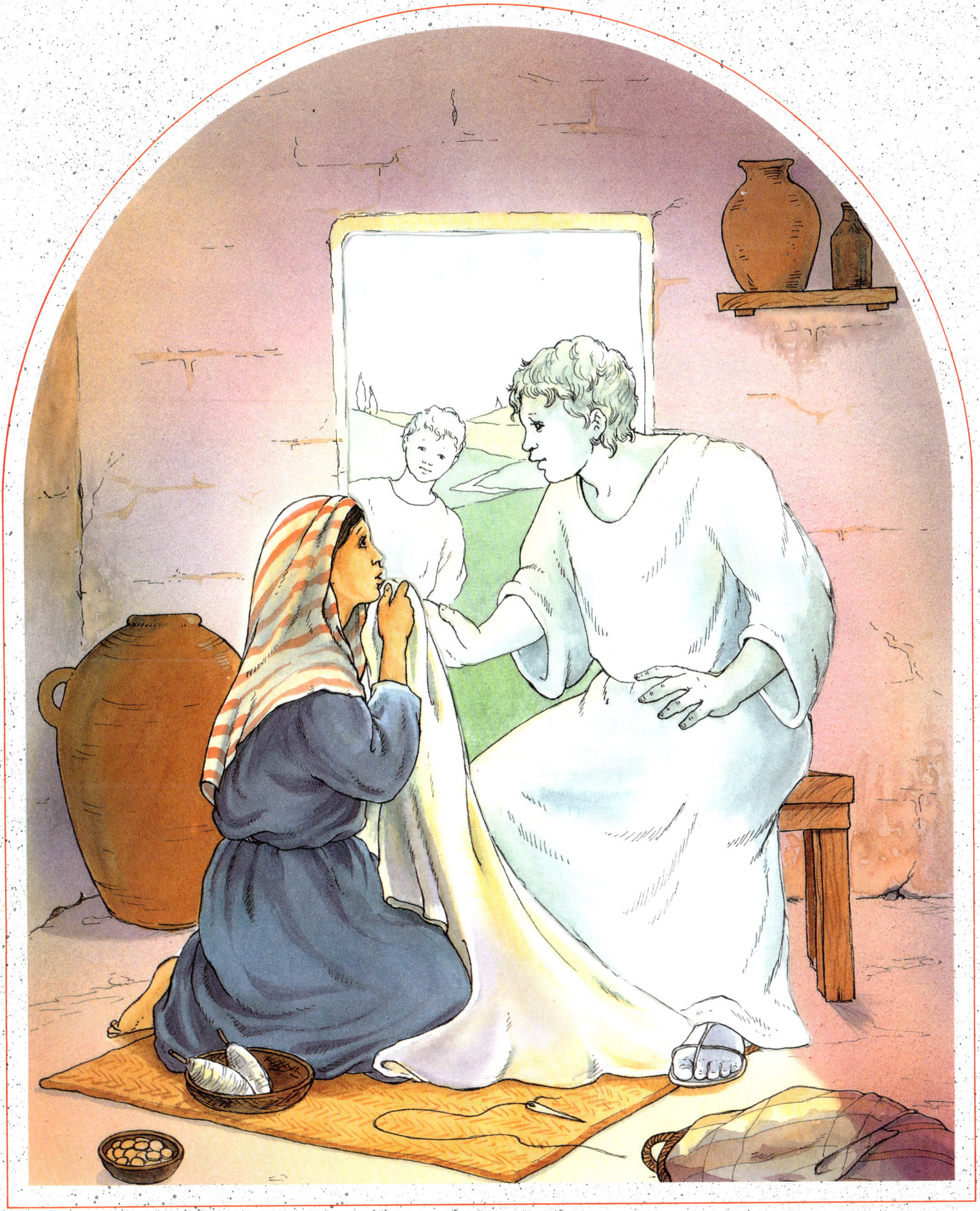

"Joseph *will* be delighted!" they told each other as they watched him hammering and sawing away in his carpenter's workshop. But they were wrong again. When Mary went to tell him about the angel, Joseph simply did not believe her.

"I can't marry you now," he said sadly. "You're telling me lies; people don't see angels these days."

Poor Mary cried as she ran home, and all the angels in heaven cried with her.

"This is terrible," they said. They knew only too well what happened if a girl had a baby when she was not married – people threw stones at her, until she died.

"That can't happen to poor Mary," sobbed the smallest angel. "Surely God will let one of us go down and talk to Joseph?" And that is just what God did. When Joseph fell asleep on the floor of his shop that night, Gabriel appeared, smiling down at him.

"Don't be frightened to marry Mary," he said. "She is telling the truth, and God wants you to be the one to help her care for His baby son, Jesus."

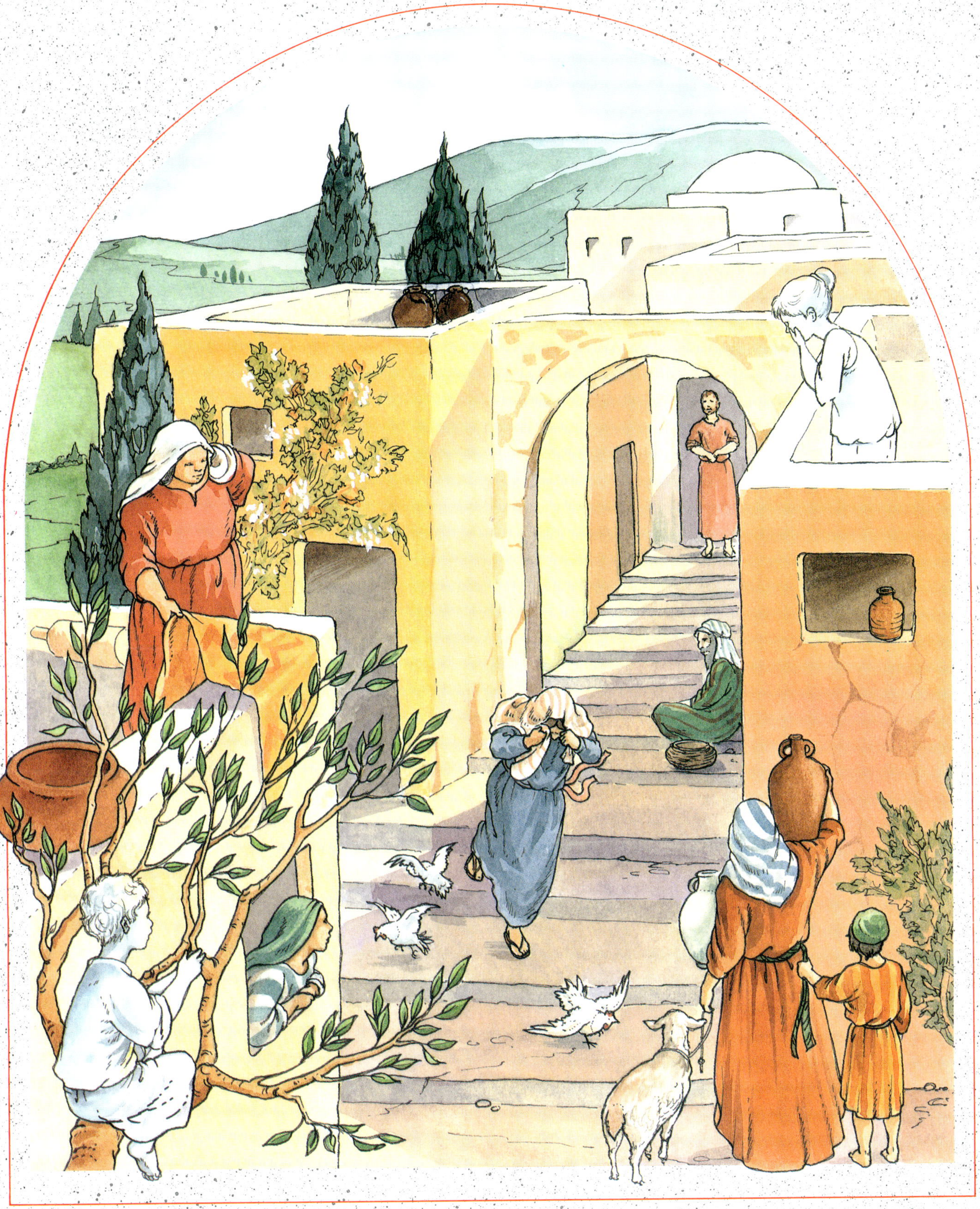

What a party the angels had the day Mary and Joseph
were married, and how happily they watched them preparing
their tiny house behind the capenter's shop.

"It's certainly not the Palace I thought God would choose
for His son's birth," muttered the smallest angel, "but Mary has
scrubbed and polished it so nicely and look at the dear little
wooden bed Joseph is making. Jesus will be safe there."

But just before Jesus was born everything went wrong.
Into the village marched a troop of Roman soldiers. They were
always ordering people around and they were so cruel no one
dared to disobey.

"You must all go back to the town where you were born so we
can count you," shouted the Captain.

"Oh, dear!" whispered Joseph. "That means we'll have to travel
a long way – right down to Bethlehem."

"What about the baby?" was all poor Mary could say.

"We have no choice," answered Joseph. "We'll have to go."

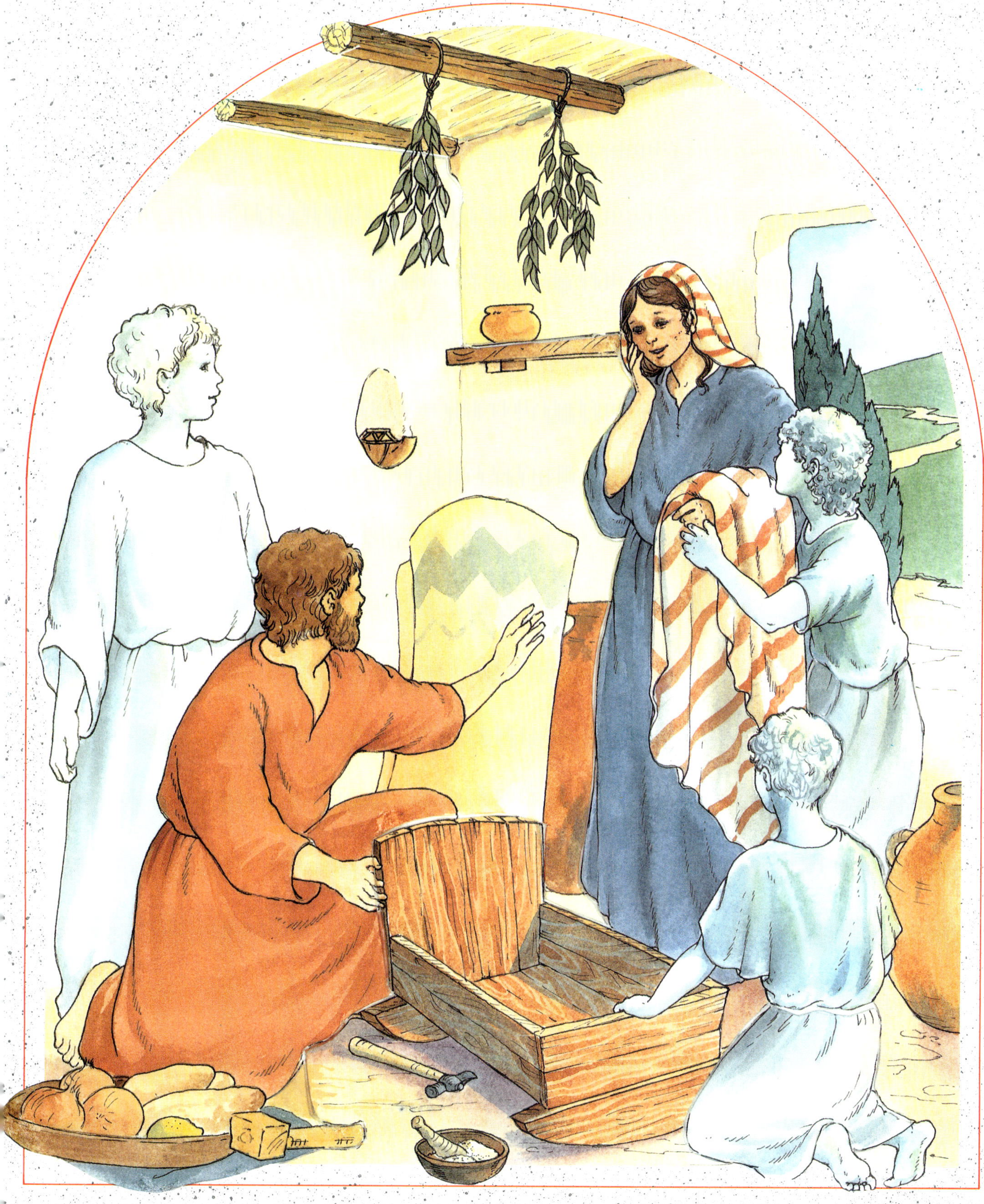

"She looks so tired," sighed the angels as they watched Mary bumping along the dusty road, mile after mile on the back of the little grey donkey.

"It will be all right when they reach Bethlehem," they told each other. There are lots of comfortable hotels and cozy houses." But how surprised they all were when Mary and Joseph finally arrived in the crowded town, late one evening. So many people had traveled there to be counted that day, there was not a bed left anywhere, and no food either.

"Go away!" said all the hotel owners, shopkeepers and housewives. "There's no room here for poor people like you." No one in Bethlehem chose to help Mary that night.

"How dare they!" The smallest angel was in tears by now. "The person who can show them how to be happy is about to be born in their town, but they're so miserable and cross they won't make room for Him."

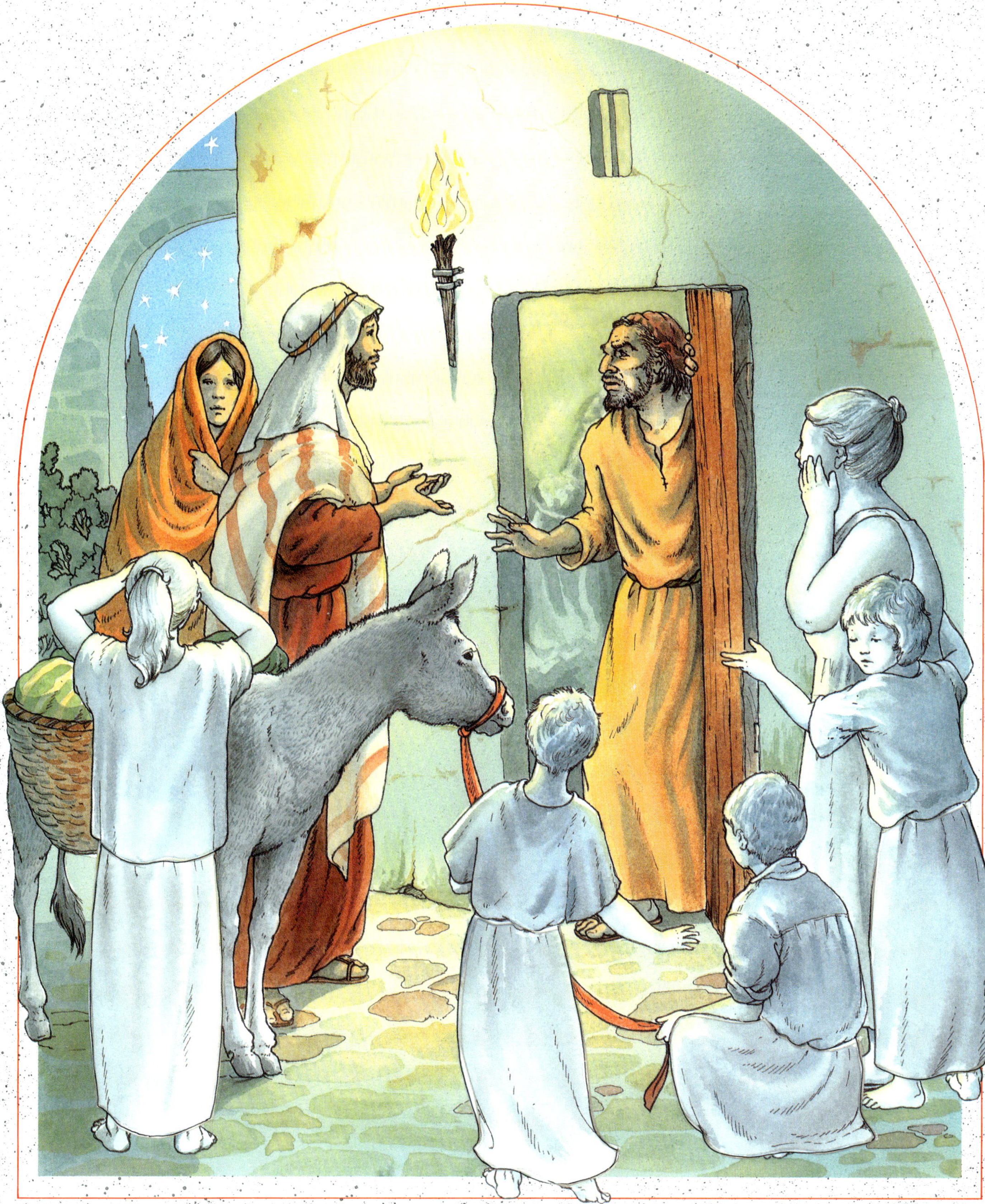

"She can't have her baby in the street," gasped the bigger angels. "He would die of cold." At last, in a back road, Joseph managed to find a dirty, tumble-down little stable and in he crept with Mary. They were cold, tired and hungry.

"Lie down on the hay," said Joseph gently. They both knew the time had come for the baby to arrive.

"How could God possibly let His son be born in a place like that!" exclaimed some of the younger angels. "Look at all those smelly farm animals; see the rats scuttling around in the rafters and the chickens scratching about the floor. Surely this must be a mistake."

"No," said Gabriel quietly, "God never makes mistakes. Jesus has gone to show what God is like, and now people who are poor, hungry or sad will always know that He understands how they feel. People often think God only loves the grand people in big palaces; now they will know He loves everyone."

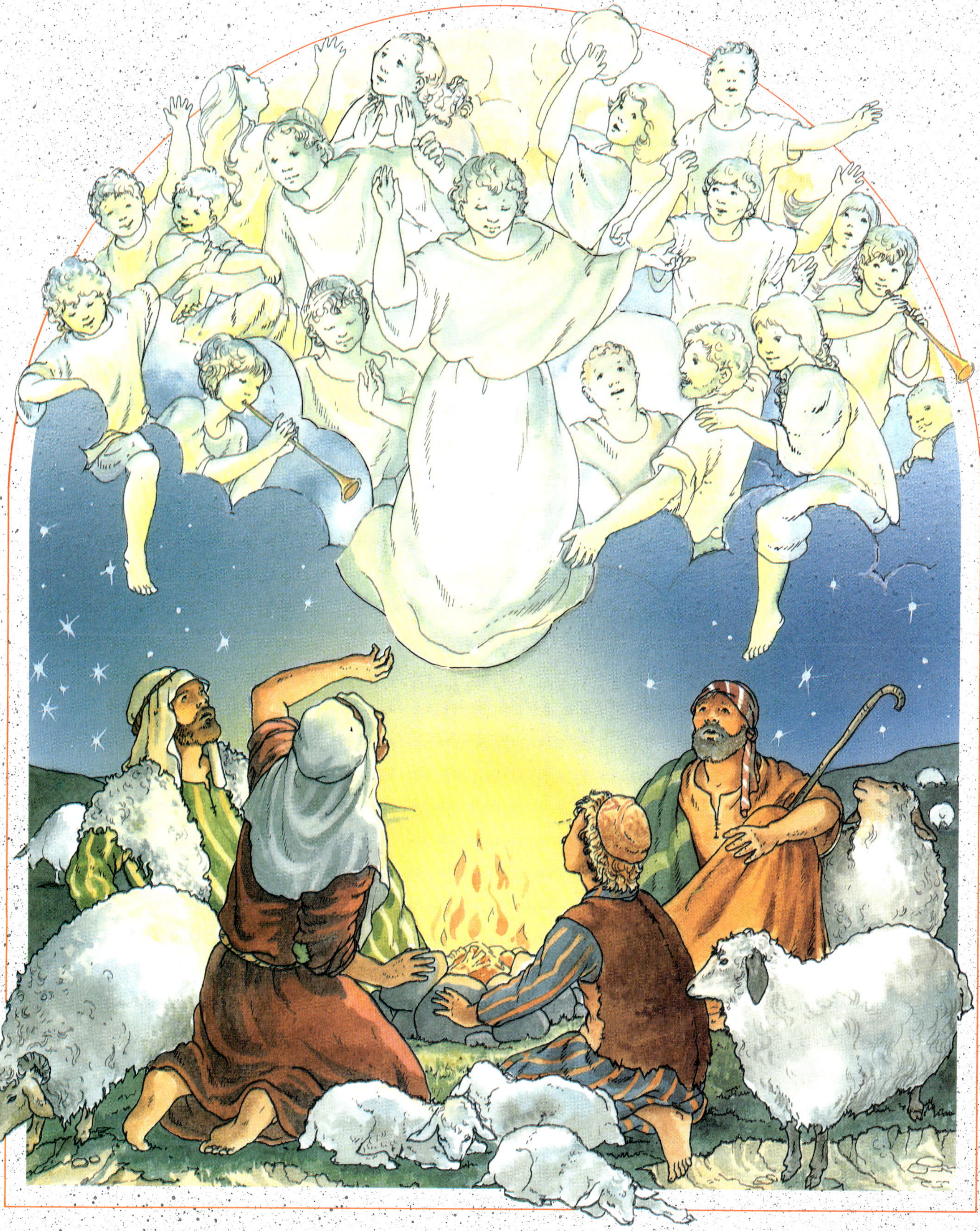

Later that night, after the baby was born,
God let the angels have a very special treat. They burst out
of heaven, filling the sky above the little town. They danced on
the clouds, clapping their hands and shouting the good news
as loudly as they could.

"Peace on earth, happiness for all men and women!"

"Now everyone will know their Someone has come at last,"
squeaked the smallest angel, who was quite hoarse from
shouting. But no one in Bethlehem bothered to look up at the
sky that night. They were all far too busy squabbling over beds
and fighting for their supper. No one noticed the angels except
a few shepherds sitting out on the hillside round their camp
fire. And they were terrified when they looked up into the
sparkling sky.

"Please don't be frightened of us," said the angels.
"We've come to tell you something so lovely. A baby has been
born for you in Bethlehem. He will save you from Satan's
power because He is Christ, the King of all the world. You will
find Him lying in a box full of hay."

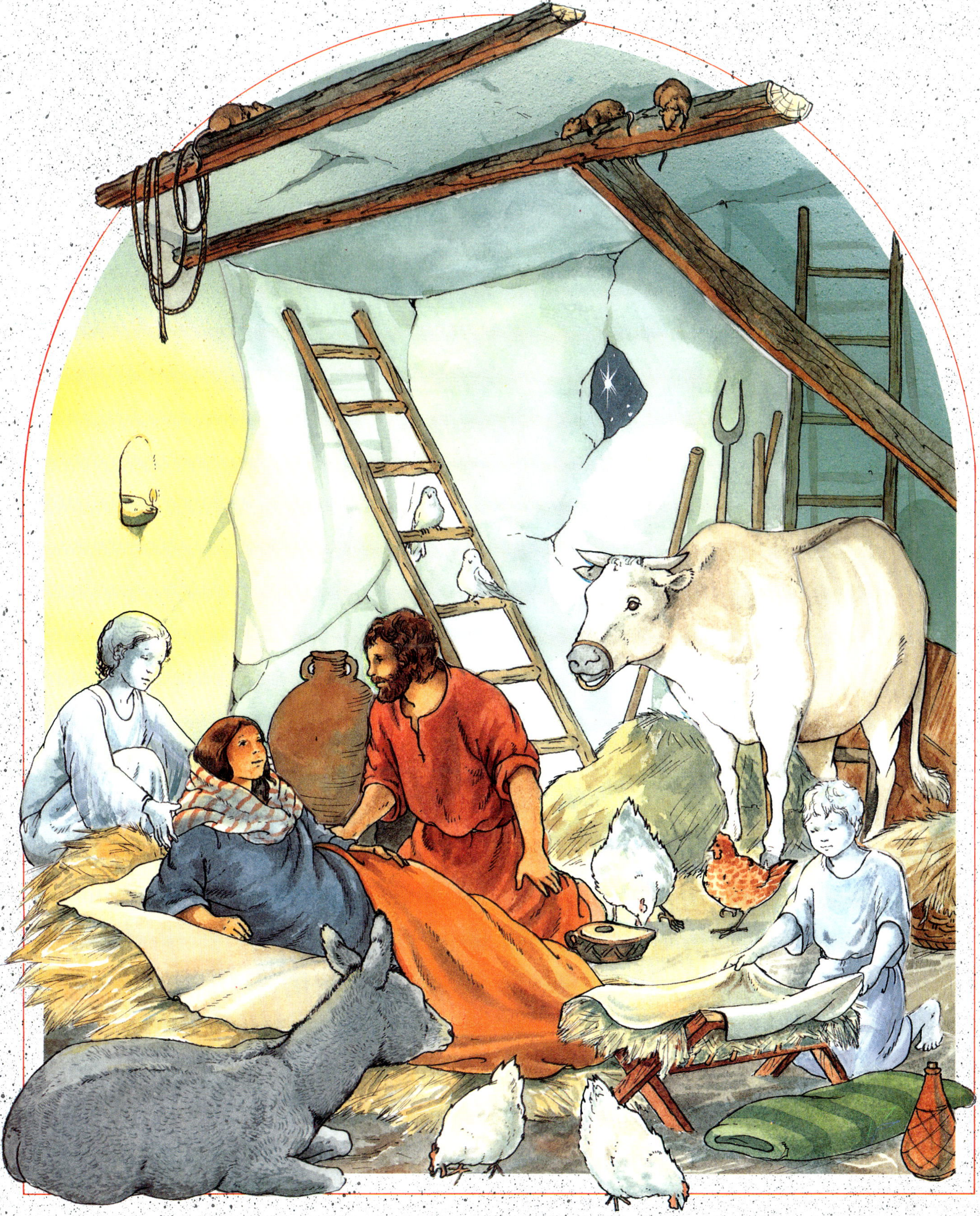

As the brightness faded gradually from the skies, the shepherds sprang up in great excitement. It did not take them long to choose to go and find Jesus! They ran off up the road to Bethlehem as fast as they could go.

"Where is He?" they shouted as they went up and down the dark streets, stumbling over the people who were trying to sleep in the shadows. "We want to see the King!" they said, startling all the cats and dogs as they peeped through cracks and doorways. Soon the whole town was awake, wanting to hear what the shepherds were saying about a sky full of angels and a King in a manger.

At last a huge crowd had gathered outside the stable where Jesus slept peacefully in the hay. "Something wonderful has happened in our town tonight," whispered all the people.

The angels were happy too, as they looked down on all the excitement. The smallest angel clapped his hands for joy when he saw the shepherds giving their best lamb to Jesus for His birthday present.

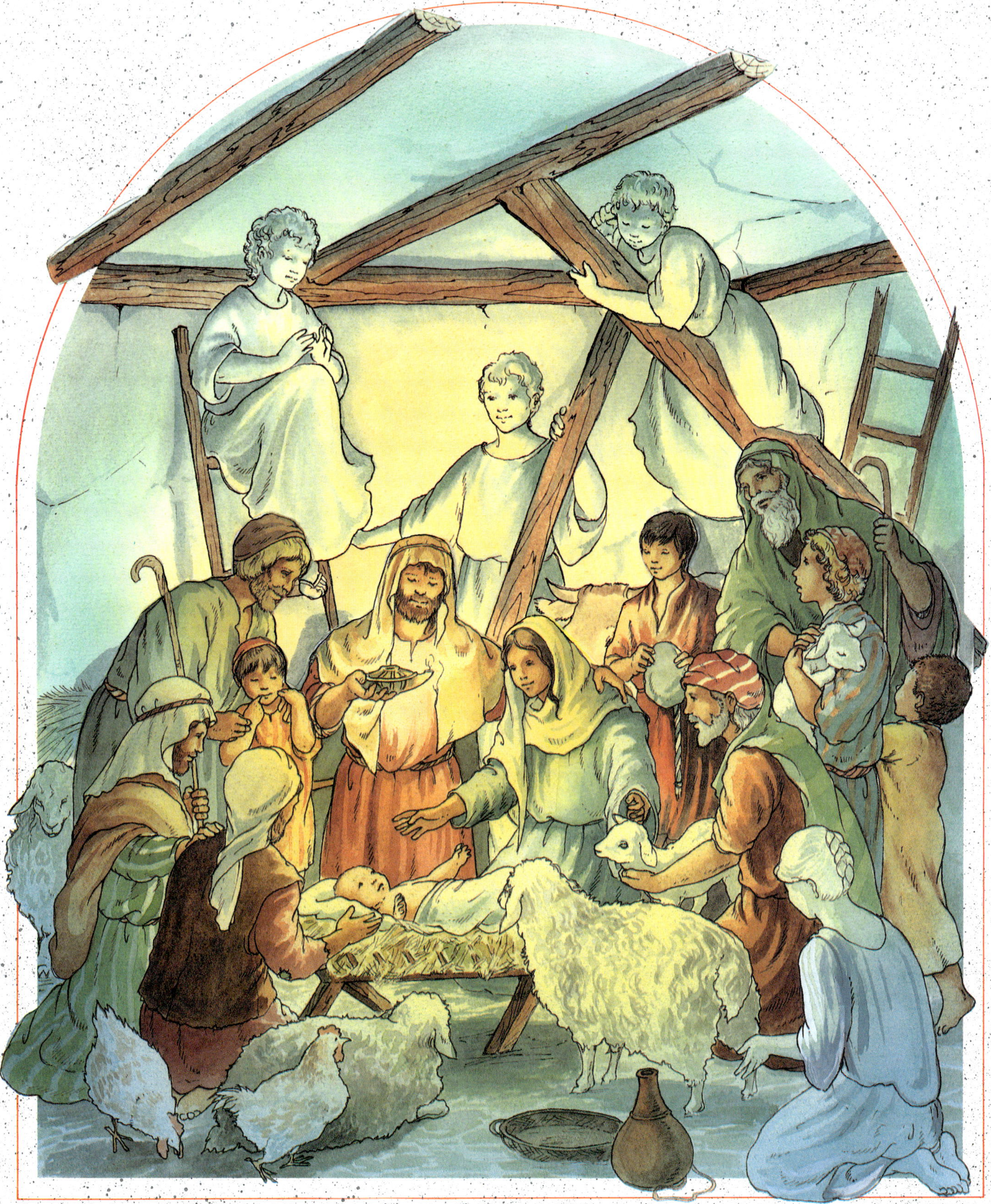

That night, God made a brand new star
to celebrate the birth of His son, and it sparkled in the sky
more brightly than all the rest. Far away in the east some wise
men looked at it in amazement. "At last!" they exclaimed.
"This is the sign we've been waiting for. It means the Special
One has come to Earth. We must go to Israel to find Him."

They mounted their camels and set off at once.
The angels were pleased as they watched the camels winding
their way across the desert, because the wise men were
bringing wonderful presents with them, fit for a baby King.

But when at last they arrived in Israel the angels began to feel
uneasy. The wise men were going in the wrong direction, and
heading straight for the palace of wicked King Herod.

"They mustn't go near him," said the smallest angel, in great
alarm. "Herod is a friend of Satan, and he'll try to harm the
baby for sure!" But it was too late— the wise men were already
knocking on the palace gate.

"Baby King!" shouted Herod furiously, "I'm the only King
round here!" Then quietly he whispered to himself, "I'm not
having some baby taking my throne."

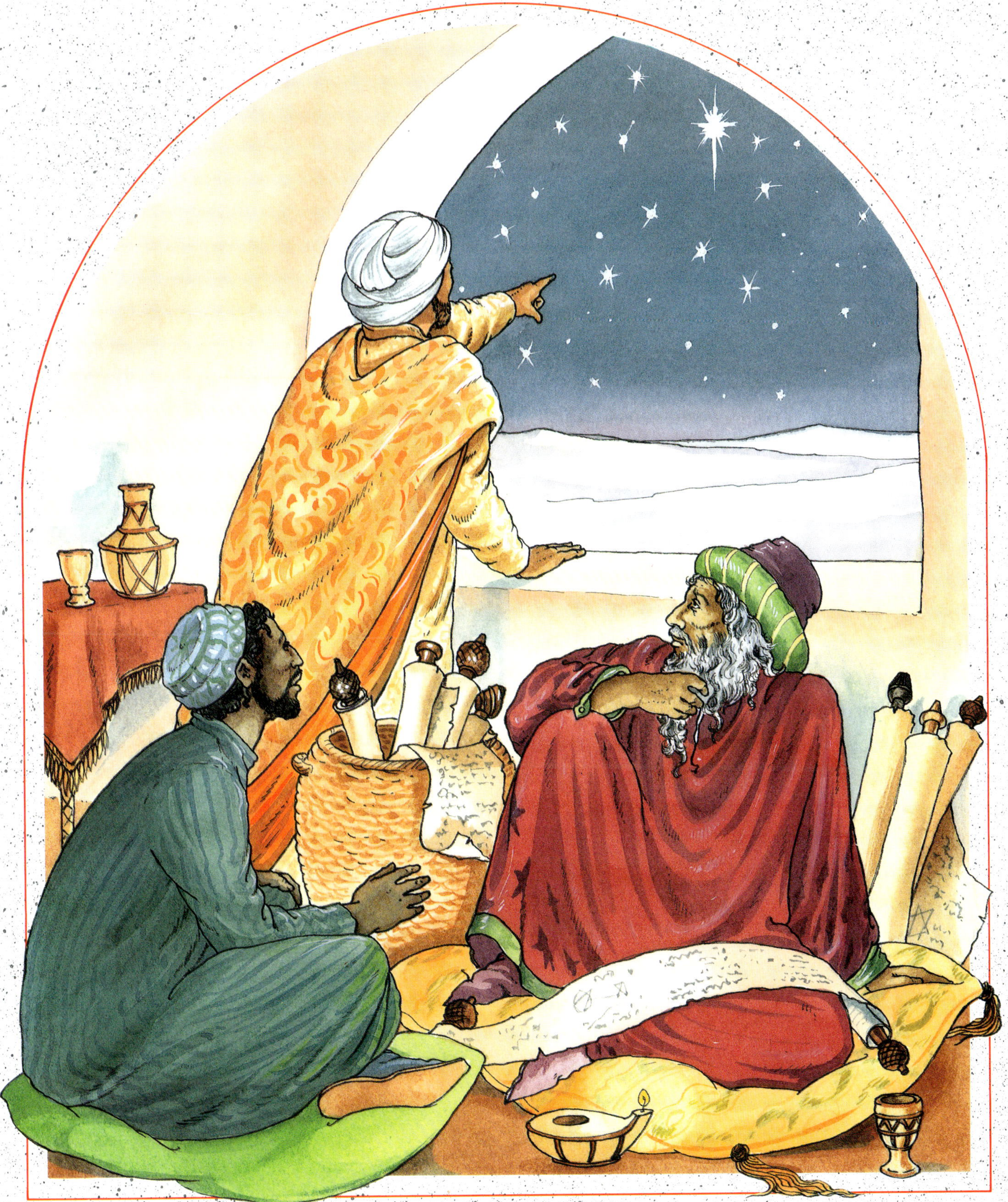

So he called his own wise men and asked them
to look in the scriptures and find out where God had said this
Special Baby would be born

"Bethlehem," they told him without delay.

"You go and find him," said Herod to his visitors,
"then come back and tell me where he is so I can go and
worship him myself."

"No! No!" cried the angels. "The clever, cunning old man.
All he wants to do is kill baby Jesus."

But after the wise men had given their presents to the baby,
God sent one of the angels to tell them not to go anywhere near
King Herod, so they hurried home on a different road. All the
angels began to smile again.

"The King will soon forget about the baby," they thought.
But Herod did not forget. Satan put a terrrible idea into his
head when he realized the wise men had tricked him. As the
angels watched in horror, King Herod called his cruel soldiers.
He sent them marching down the road to kill all the children
in Bethlehem.

Satan rubbed his hands together in glee as he watched the
moonlight glint on their sharp swords and the daggers in their
belts. He was pleased with the thought that Jesus would never
grow up to be the proof of God's love and show people the
way to Heaven.

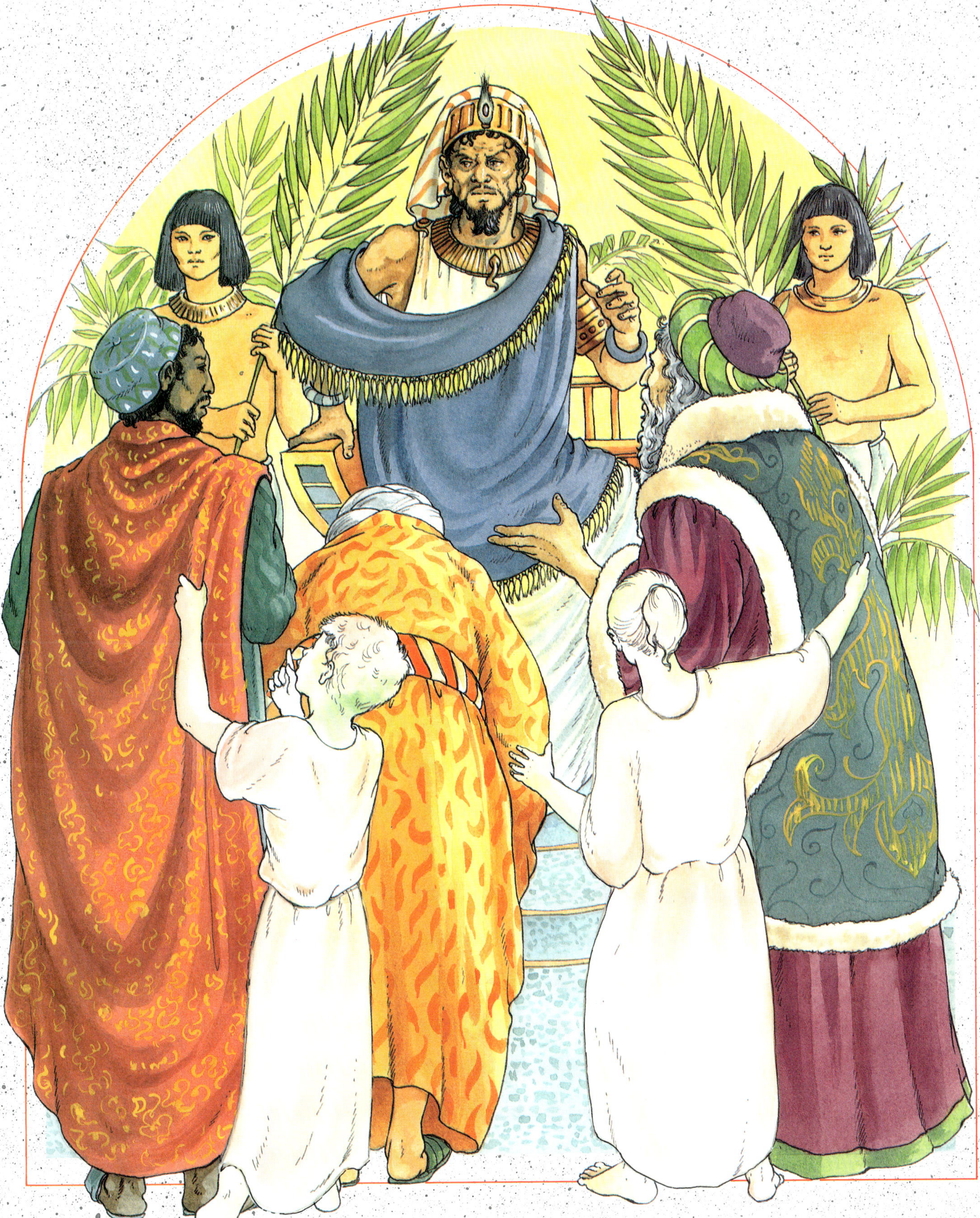

Joseph was sleeping peacefully, with Mary and Jesus cuddled up beside him. They did not know that every minute the soldiers were marching nearer and nearer through the darkness of the night. Then, suddenly, God beckoned to Gabriel and whispered something in his ear and the great angel sped down to earth with yet another message.

He had to shake Joseph to wake him up.
"Quick! Quick!" Gabriel said. "You must escape at once. Soldiers are on their way here to kill the Son of God. Go to the faraway land of Egypt and stay there until wicked Herod is safely dead and buried."

◇

Nearer and nearer marched the soldiers' heavy feet, but just as they reached the main gate of the town, a little grey donkey slipped quietly out into the safety of the hills. On his back sat Mary holding her sleepy baby, and Joseph walked along beside them.

"Just in time!" The smallest angel breathed a sigh of relief. "Now Jesus can grow up to tell people how to be God's friends. He will show them what God is like, and they will be able to join us in Heaven by following Him. How wonderful of God to have defeated Satan by sending His own Son as a baby. But it's just as well God had our help to look after them all!"

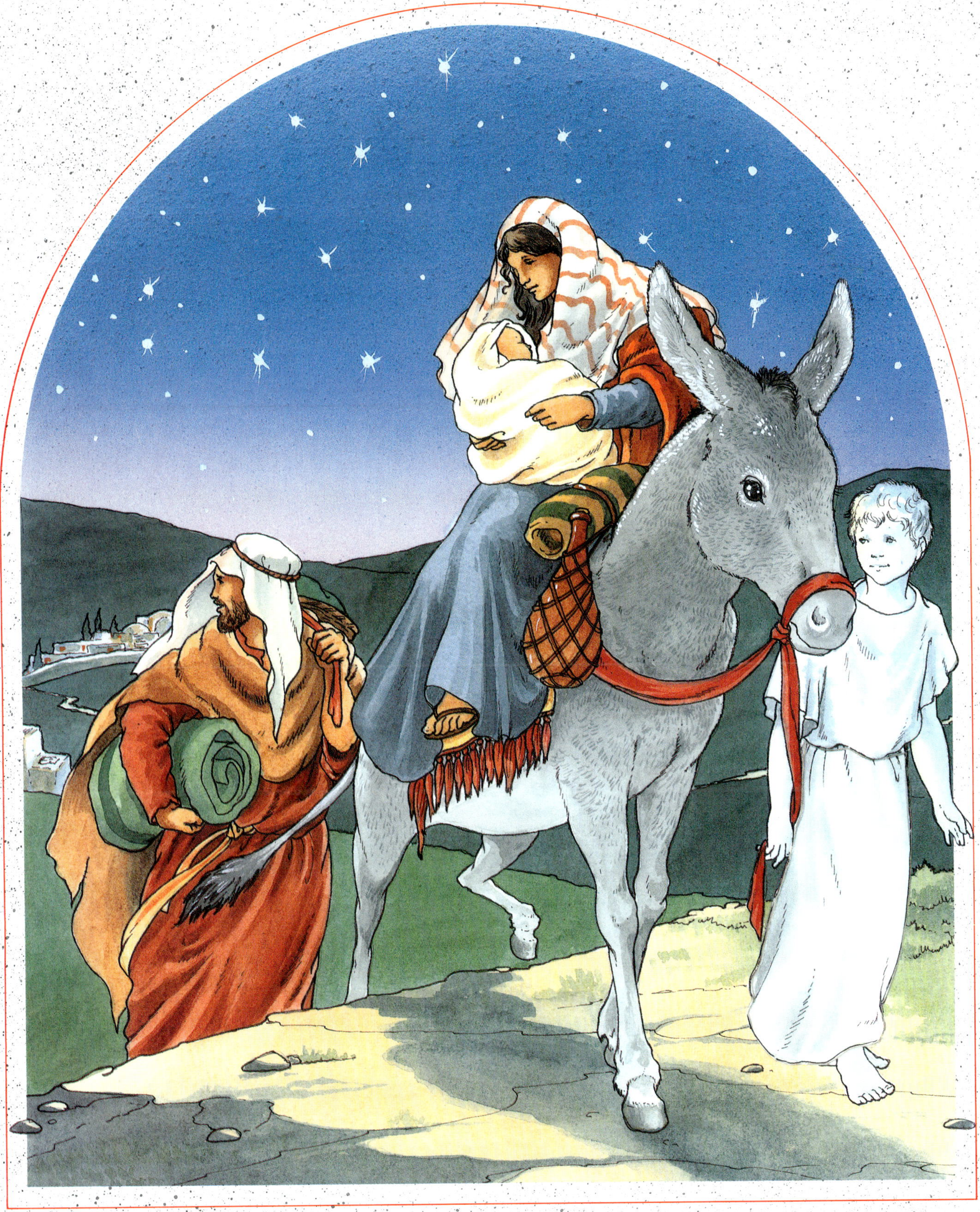

Copyright © 1991 Hunt and Thorpe
Text © Jennifer Larcombe Rees
Illustrations © Maggie Downer
Originally published by Hunt and Thorpe 1991
ISBN 1 85608 028 5

All rights reserved. Except for brief quotations in
critical articles or reviews, no part of this book may be
reproduced in any manner without prior permission from
the publishers. Write to: Hunt and Thorpe,
66 High St, Alton, Hants GU34 1ET.

Manufactured in Singapore.